John Osborne was born in Sc  author of three non-fiction *Newsagent's Window* and *Don* poems are often heard on the r.   ... is a regular at festivals including Latitude, Glastonbury and Port Eliot. His debut solo show *John Peel's Shed* enjoyed a sell-out run at the Edinburgh Festival in 2011 and was adapted for broadcast on BBC Radio 4. He co-organises Homework, a night of literary miscellany in East London. This is his first full poetry collection. Find him at johnosbornewriter.com

Most People Aren't
That Happy, Anyway

John Osborne

Nasty Little Press

Published by Nasty Little Press in January 2013.

Nasty Little Press
35 St Johns Road, Bungay, Suffolk, NR35 1DH
nastylittlepress.org
@nastylit

ISBN: 978-0-9573000-4-0

Set in Book Antiqua. Printed and bound by MPG Biddles

A CIP record of this book is available
from the British Library.

Cover illustration by Sam Ratcliffe.

Contents

Listening to Stuart Maconie, 1

Surprise!, 2

Screaming our tits off, 4

When you were talking about your mum, 6

Me and my sister, 7

Most people aren't that happy, anyway, 9

Skiing accident, 11

Hoops, 12

Sinead O'Connor, 13

Airdrie United, 15

We should call a man, 17

George Alagiah, 19

A few nice billionaires, 21

That money would have turned you into a bastard, 22

A boy called Michael Jackson, 24

He was unsuccessful and then he died, 26

Grown man makes new friend, 27

The Hooters waitress, 29

Drunk groom, 31

Citizen's arrest, 33

Tuesday was my perfect day, 35

A poem for Simon Armitage, 37

A day in the life, 39

The continuity announcer stole my wife, 44

I wish I believed in aliens, 46

Both Grandmas, 48

Apocalypse, 49

Je joue le ping pong, 51

A secret something, 53

The boy and girl busking on Hastings seafront, 55

The 2009 Cannes film festival, 58

Soya milk, 59

Schmoozing at an evening do, 60

A pair of last year's trousers, 61

Listening to Radio 3 in the bath, 63

Our waitress is the employee of the month, 64

MOST PEOPLE AREN'T THAT HAPPY, ANYWAY

"Out of the millions of people we live among, most of whom we habitually ignore and are ignored by in turn, there are always a few who hold hostage our capacity for happiness, whom we could recognise by their smell alone and whom we would rather die than be without."

Alain de Botton

"You never feel more alive than when hiding under a bed."

Danny Baker

Listening to Stuart Maconie

You shout out crossword clues
while I iron my work shirts.
It's payday tomorrow
and there's a stack of DVDs we ordered from Amazon
that we still haven't watched.
and Stuart Maconie is on the radio. You like him.
We've SkyPlus'd The Apprentice
it's only two weeks until we go to New York
and the chicken is nearly roasted.

Our friends will be here soon.
We've a case of red wine to get through
and a massive Toblerone.
Stuart Maconie has just played Whippin' Piccadilly
and if it's still sunny at eight o'clock
we can drink gin-and-tonics in the garden
and tell everyone that Katie called this afternoon
to say she's expecting twins in September.

But as I sit waiting for our guests to arrive
I can't help but look at the patio doors
and think 'What if men burst in wearing balaclavas?'
and imagine an elbow through the glass
a man holding a gun in your mouth
while I am told to fill a bag
with our valuables.

Surprise!

It's you I feel sorry for.
You hired the room
and when no-one RSVP'd
you assumed my friends were too cool to RSVP
so ordered a finger buffet for fifty.
My surprise birthday party:
four of us,
me and you, your mum and dad.
When I told you once I don't like the idea of surprise parties
this was the kind of thing I had in mind.

"Maybe I put the wrong date on the invitations," you said,
as the waiter offered us yet more crabsticks.
We both knew you'd have triple-checked.
"Not even Graham," you said.
"Graham plays squash on Wednesdays," I said
and blew out the candles on the cake.

Under the table were bottles of wine,
thirty red and thirty white.
There wasn't even the chance to get a refund;
the receipt was in your handbag
that had been snatched that morning.

By the time we sang the happy birthday song
the waiter was so pissed he'll probably be fired
but anyone who can dance like that
is wasted in catering.

"What's it like not to have any friends?" your dad asked
and we all laughed apart from your mum
who still had her coat on.
"Maybe there's something good on the telly," he said.
I've never liked your dad
but last night he played a blinder
juggling satsumas as we looked out of the window.

It wasn't a special birthday.
I was 29, a prime number.
No-one gets excited about prime numbers,
but it reminded me of the time I was at Graham's house
when I pulled down my trousers and pants
and showed everyone the massive bruise on my knob.
I just thought more people would be interested.

Screaming our tits off

Our clothes in a bundle near dogs chasing dogs
our footprints in the direction of the water.
At first I was worried about my new trainers being stolen
and dying,
but as soon as we'd shouted 1, 2, 3 and ran
into waves taller than basketball players
we no longer had the ability to control things,
could do nothing but scream our bank statements away.
All worries about exes and bad backs and career choices
had been left on the beach
tucked up with our socks in the toes of our shoes
as we unleashed toxins from our ribcages.

The ocean is the opposite of traffic jams.
In the sea you have never felt further away
from the Costa's queue at Welcome Break.
When our heads were underwater we entered a world
without A roads and mini roundabouts.
The only thing that mattered was survival.
We've all heard those stories
about people who did a fun thing and then died
and we were dancing with hypothermia,
that odd contradiction of screaming your tits off
with the tranquillity of breaststroke.

Swimming has always been my happy place
ever since those days of me and my dad
walking to the leisure centre on Saturday mornings,
a 25 metre badge sewn on my cloth bag.
I was prouder of that than any degree
and we were in the sea for maybe a minute,
ninety seconds max, before swimming back, grabbing our stuff,
legging it to the disabled toilets to get changed
and as we dried our hair under the hand dryers
goosepimples disappeared under my jumper.

When you were talking about your mum

It sounded like you were close
your mum, your dad and you.
You told me about holidays on the beach
and the birthday parties they gave you.
I really wanted to ask
'how old were you when ...'

but figured you wouldn't want to talk about that day
and it was too early in our relationship for that kind of thing.
That night when we went to bed
it was the first time we just went to bed
instead of either of us saying
'let's go to bed.'

Me and my sister

I had a dream that me and my sister were in a car crash. We both died, but carried on being alive inside cuddly toys. We were for sale in a toy shop, a little boy came in with his mum and she told him he could pick any two toys, and even though me and my sister were far apart from each other on the shelves, we were the two he chose.

He carried us home, one under each arm. He put us in his bedroom and when he went downstairs and closed the door behind him it was like when we had to share a bedroom at Christmas because Grandma had come to stay. We would stay up late talking, too excited to go to sleep. And so in the little boy's room me and my sister just hung out, the way we have always done. She said 'remember when we were little and had baths together and you used to drink the bathwater.' She said 'I bet all our primary school teachers are dead by now' and I thought about Mrs Cooper and Mr Thompson and realised she was probably right. We talked about people we worked with when we both had summer jobs at Safeway. We talked about how we watched every episode of Big Brother 3 and were pleased when Kate Lawler won. She reminded me she always beat me at board games. I reminded her I was faster than her at front crawl.

Neither of us mentioned that we were both dead now and had become cuddly toys, but it didn't really matter, because we were together, just me and my sister, and that's the way we liked it best. The little boy came back into his room and gave us a cuddle. I was Eeyore. Karen was a dog called Patch.

Most people aren't that happy, anyway

He buttons up his coat, walks to his car;
that transitory period between being a man at work
to putting coins into the hospital car park meter.

The first time he mentioned his son
on a kidney dialysis machine,
I thought: well that explains why sometimes I look up from my desk
and see him playing solitaire on his computer
letting the phone ring and ring.

Sometimes he'll come into the office and say "What's up, slags?"'
He'll say "What are you doing here Colin, you muppet?"
or "Why don't you return my calls, you pillock?"
and I always thought 'What a dick,'
but you can't judge people by what they do and say,
it's the way they sigh when they sit down on their chair.

Most people aren't that happy,
they're arguing about Iraq on internet forums
or phoning work at 9.05. "I've overslept again.
I'll be there as soon as I can."
They're asking if their spectacles have been handed in at lost property,
they're at How To Quit Smoking seminars in church halls
or on the settee, waiting for their favourite programme to start,
not realising the series ended last week.

Of course there are people who have made it
Assistant Producers at Radio 1, waitresses at The Ivy,
Holly Branson,
but most people aren't that happy
and no-one is going to say "Oh look, a portal,"
and you can close your eyes and jump
into a time before you lost your glasses,
when it was all four of you at home,
when you didn't forget to put the oven on
before you went for that walk
on Christmas afternoon.

Skiing Accident

On his last day on the slopes
he runs into the bar
his thumb cradled in his cupped hands.

It is like a hitch hiker
in an avalanche
as the barmaid fills a bucket with crushed ice.

She smiles as she phones for an ambulance
He'd been there all week, ordering drinks
clicking his fingers.

Hoops

He goes down on one knee,
the crowd holds its breath
like when a player shapes to shoot
in the dying seconds
of the final quarter.

She shakes her head
runs to the emergency exit
and the crowd watches him
get back to his feet.
He puts the ring back in his inside pocket
as he's led off
comforted by a giant mouse.

The players are back on court
trying to pretend nothing has happened.
The ball bounces off the hoop
goes out of touch.

Sinead O'Connor

Nothing compares to you.
I know this song already exists. Written by Prince
as people are always quick to point out
but with you it's true.
Nothing compares to you.

I am saying that. Not crooning it like O'Connor
this isn't parody or a late night pissed up singalong.
Nothing compares to you.

I knew you would break my heart.
"She'll break your heart," your friends warned
usually unsolicited
although sometimes I'd be mischievous and say
"Everything will be okay between us?"
which always prompted a comforting arm on my shoulder.
"You need to be careful with her."

Being cheated on is like being mugged
where the only thing in your wallet is your library card,
the phone number of someone quite important,
a photo of the dog we saw in the street once
and the first shopping list we ever wrote together
that I have inexplicably kept. No use to thieves.

I knew you would break my heart.
I just liked being near you.
Probably deep down I deserve this
but right now, I just think how nothing compares to you
and imagine you opening my wallet
to find no cash or bank card,
just my sort of smiling face on my driving licence
the photograph of that massive dog
and the shopping list.
"He kept the shopping list," you'll say.

Airdrie United

The top scorer in the Scottish Third Division
is called Ryan Donnelly
and I want to know how he feels when he scores
if he launches himself into the home fans
if he performs backwards somersaults
or just jogs back over the centre circle.

I want to know if he's got a girlfriend
I want to know if she keeps cuttings of him from the local newspapers
I want to know if his dad sits in the Director's Box
reminiscing of the days he spent walking up and down the touchline
of the muddy school field
before driving him home for his tea.

I want to know how he feels when he wakes up in the morning
knowing he's going to spend the whole day
practising scoring headers from corners
sprinting in-between orange cones.
I want to know if he gets recognised in the supermarket
I want to know if people walk around town wearing replica shirts
with his name on the back.

I want to know if he's mates with the goalie
I want to know if he's good at keepy uppies
I want to watch him do the Cruyff turn

I want to know if he's ever grieved over the death of a grandparent
I want to know if he practices taking penalties
I want to know if he did anything special on Pancake Day
I want to know if he's read Gianluca Vialli's autobiography
I want to know if he swears at referees
I want to know if he has trouble with his hamstrings.

We should call a man

The bonnet of our Punto
is propped open with a wooden spoon.
My face and shirt are smudged with oil,
bits of engine are scattered across the front lawn
like childrens' toys.
You stand on the doorstep
with your arms folded, and say:
"We need to get a man in."

In our shed is a Flymo edge trimmer,
a Black & Decker Jigsaw,
a Bosh cordless screwdriver
still in their boxes
lined up like *Star Wars* collectables;
because whenever something goes wrong
you shake your head and I know you're thinking
of the time I tried to fix the washing machine
and flooded the utility room.

And when I fixed the guttering
the ladder fell to the floor. I had to wait on the roof
until you came home.
So when something needs doing
you say "We need to get a man in."

The stubs in my chequebook
read: *Man*
Man
Man
Man

There's a man in our living room now
trying to install a wireless connection.
He has been in there for two hours.
I take him a cup of tea
and see: his head in his hands, instruction book
thrown to the floor. Suddenly
we are equals.

George Alagiah

Every day George Alagiah practices saying the same line:
the Queen is Dead
the Queen is Dead
the Queen is Dead.

He says it into the mirror when shaving,
sings it in the shower,
enunciates every word when driving to work,
"We have some breaking news:
the Queen is dead."

He rehearses scenarios:
"She died peacefully in her sleep."
"She was hit by a bullet in a drive-by."
"She was killed in a car crash in Paris."

George Alagiah's wife has not been on holiday for years.
Her suggestions of a week in Spain are ignored
brochures of Tuscany are thrown in the bin
there is no chance of a weekend city break.

George knows the value of full attendance
he does not want to give anyone else
the chance to say the words,
not Huw Edwards, Fiona Bruce,
Sophie Raworth.

Whenever they see each other in the BBC canteen
they just glare.
They all know what the other is thinking,
they want to be the one to break the news.
"If you are just tuning in
the Queen is dead."

George Alagiah has a bag packed especially
he keeps it by the front door.
In it is a black tie, a comb,
a notebook with a carefully worded eulogy.

Every time he goes to bed
he knows his sleep could be disturbed by the phone ringing
and it will be his producer saying "George,
something terrible has happened.
We need you."

A few nice billionaires

My friend Nelson goes out every day
feeding the ducks at the pond near the old Woolworths.
I think maybe he's worked out something
that the rest of us haven't.
Newlyweds asleep on a hammock
oblivious to what one politician just called another
during *Prime Minister's Questions*.

Why can't we say from now on all debts are wiped,
all money counts double,
shops can accept photocopied fivers.
Let's treat the world economy
like a past-his-bedtime-seven-year-old playing Monopoly
just throw it on the floor
hope someone else picks up the pieces.

All we need is a few nice billionaires
to put their hands in their pockets.
They'd get a little glow inside.
The cock-a-hoop homeless man at the recycling bin:
"I won't be needing this piece of cardboard anymore.
I've got an en suite at an eccentric's house.
He's lent me his favourite book.
Bought me an electric toothbrush.
Turns out he's glad to have the company."

That money would have turned you into a bastard

You found out when you saw your friends and colleagues
on the front page of the local newspaper
shaking hands with the newsagent
who sold them the winning ticket
being presenting with a novelty cheque.

But I promise it will turn out to be for the best
that you didn't put a pound in Greg's tin
and said "I'm in,"
like you had done every week for the last eight years.
Those begging letters would start to get annoying
although it is always nice to get something in the post.

Remember, last year, going on holiday to Morocco,
queuing at Gatwick the excitement
was because you knew you had earned it,
all those lunch breaks you sat at your computer
because if you didn't, the work just wouldn't get done.

Or when that barmaid gave you too much change
and you didn't say anything
because she's always been such a bitch;
that feeling of paying with a fiver
and getting £6.20 back, and a pint;
that feeling of excitement in your stomach,

like a drunk man who has just found a xylophone,
that would be lost forever.

So I don't blame you for deciding to opt out,
of course you were never going to win,
nothing good ever happens to you.
There's as much chance of you being hit on the head
by a double bass, falling from the sky
than matching the Thunderball.
This way you could save £52 a year.
You can have a good night out for that
go out for a massive curry
or maybe get a subscription to Viz,
or buy four brand new DVDs.

The rest of the syndicate
will have moved into their mansions by now
they'll be racing quad bikes around their estates
as their fancy kitchens are being built.
It must feel you're the only one not invited
to a party that lasts forever.
You're Pete Best and they're The Beatles
getting off the plane at JFK
but remember this:
rich people are dicks
and that money would have turned you into a bastard.

A boy called Michael Jackson

I used to play chess with a boy called Michael Jackson.
He wasn't very good at chess
but that was the least of his problems.
And I've always felt sorry for him
unable to answer the most basic question:
"What's your name?"
"Michael Jackson."
Imagine the quips. Especially now.
"I thought you were dead!"

He can't even make a simple phone call,
ringing up the BT Helpdesk
they say "Can I take your name?"
He says "Michael Jackson,"
and there's a pause and he says
"Yes, like the singer.
No, you're not the first person to mention it.
Yes, it can be quite annoying.
No, I don't know what my parents were thinking,
I guess they weren't familiar with the Jackson 5.
My dad works 50 hours a week as a neurosurgeon
and my mum is a full time carer for her brother
who has Down's Syndrome,
I guess they're too busy to listen to disco."

When he first started to go to clubs
the bouncer would check his driving licence,
call over to his mate: "This one's called Michael Jackson!"
At the airport, the man in the passport booth says
"Can you do the moonwalk?"
and Michael Jackson says "No,
I'm just going on holiday with my wife,"
and he'll say "What, Lisa Marie Presley?"
"No, her name's Anne. Anne Jackson.
Try making a joke out of that."

There must be thousands of people
going through the same tedious conversations,
people called James Bond,
Harry Potter, Steve Davis, Mark Thatcher,
Dennis Taylor, Katie Price, Alan Bennett, Fred West,
and little Michael Jackson
who says "No, I'm not the singer.
I'm just here for a game of chess."

He was unsuccessful and then he died

He spent most of his time
reading coffee table books about paintings.

He loved art.
He thought he was good at it

and there's nothing he'd have liked more
than an exhibition of his own work

the knowledge that a stranger
could see one of his landscapes

in a nice big wooden frame
think 'I like that' and pay their money.

It would hang on the bedroom wall
of these newlyweds who were furnishing their house

they knew nothing about art
just loved the simplicity of this painting.

"This is exactly what we were looking for,"
they'd have said.

Grown man makes new friend

"How are you keeping?" he asks
once they've chosen a beer from the chalkboard
of the Camra shortlisted Pub of the Year
that's worth the extra walk.

After their third pint he takes out his plastic bag
gives back the CDs he borrowed
the last time he went round for a coffee
now burnt onto his Dell.

He listens to them every night
in the room that used to be his office
in his comfy chair
with his slightly-too-expensive-to-justify headphones
and a four pack from the local shop.
"My treat," he tells himself
but the man behind the counter seems very familiar.
Nice newsagent. One of the best he's had.

"Well I suppose we better invite him round for his tea,"
his wife says when she noticed Paul's name
continually dropped into conversation:
"Paul's got the same secateurs as us."
"Paul and his wife have got a cleaner."
"Your handwriting's a bit like Paul's."

27

As Paul helps himself to an extra roast potato
it turns out they both liked cricket,
arrange to go to a match together.
It seems so long since he'd had this:
nice wine with dinner, then opening the bottle of port
saying "Do you like Jefferson Airplane?"
and then Jefferson Airplane play on the five disc changer
as his wife gets the cheese out.

And the more complicated the music gets
the emptier the bottle of port.
Paul says "Did you sort that problem at work?"
"Was it okay at the doctors?"
"Just pay me back when you can."

He can't remember the last time
he stored a new number in his phone,
that anyone gave him advice on jeans.
It's like the time he heard that song on the radio
kept singing it
found out the name of the band
went by himself to watch them live
ordered the whole back catalogue.

The Hooters waitress

I think I imagined it like this:
our dog in front of us chasing a stick,
you still in your Hooters uniform,
the breeze tousling your peroxide pigtails.

I have come to meet you on your lunch break.
I do this every day, bring the dog with me,
we walk along the beach
stop and get something to eat.
They used to give us funny looks, but not now.
They're used to us in our regular cafe
you in your Lycra, stirring your cup of tea,
reading a magazine, talking to me about your day.

"She's not a stripper," I explain to my grandparents,
but admit it's not dissimilar.
And no I don't mind that men stare.
If I was married to Zadie Smith
I'd want everyone to read *White Teeth*.

"You should see us on our days off," I tell my friends
who ask what's it like to be engaged to a Hooters waitress.
"There's no glamour. We do jigsaws in our pyjamas."
I tell them about your Neighbourhood Watch meetings:
estate agents, primary school teachers, greengrocers

and a Hooters waitress, all worried
about what the council are planning to do
with the plot of land round the corner.

"We'll open a florists with the money you make
on tips from businessmen,"
I suggest, when we start to plan a family
and are worried about our children having to admit
their mum wears hot-pants for a living.
"You can work in the shop and I'll do the deliveries,
or the other way round if you prefer,"
I would still pander to her, even at this stage
me and the waitress from Hooters.

Drunk Groom

It will not surprise you to learn
he is no longer wearing his little dickie bow,
he took that off before he'd even started his soup.

He unbuttoned his shirt completely
for the photograph of him with his mates from uni,
with his mother in law's mother and all the barstaff
during the wella *Wella wella oomph* of the *Grease* medley.

All those nights he'd spent at Chicago Rock Café
hoping there might be a fittie
chatting up girls in bookshops
have accumulated in uniting these two families.
The best day of their lives they kept saying
on the lawn
drinking Pimms with the Beacocks.

And he knew that as he was saying "I do,"
Gordon, a man with a van,
was moving everything into their new home.
He was being paid a grand in cash to do the job lot
which meant the next morning
they could head straight from the honeymoon suite
to their new place
a happily married couple.
Wella wella wella oomph.

Which is why no-one minded that all evening
his breath smelled a bit of puke
that he smashed a champagne flute, didn't tell anyone
and both bridesmaids cut their feet.
His woozy new wife had a cigarette outside
at first she ignored the conga
but joined it the second time round.

Citizen's Arrest

I am sitting on a man!

I saw the bag-snatch and normally I'd have looked the other way.
This is not the kind of thing I do.

I am a very boring man.
I wear my normal clothes to fancy dress parties.

When my bus is late I don't mind
I'm happy to sit on the bench

but for some reason this time
I shouted STOP and ran

and now I've got my knee in this guy's back.
The lady can't stop saying thank-you.

She says there are some details in her address book
which would have been lost forever.

She tells me she doesn't have much in her purse,
but tries to put together a reward

I refuse it, which she expects.
We both know how this kind of thing works.

I don't even feel scared
as I wave at passers by

tightening the armlock with my other hand.
I'm like a muddy boy with a tadpole in a jam jar

curious about this creature wriggling.

Tuesday was my perfect day

"Tuesday was my perfect day, by the way," you told me
and I thought 'well that's going to stop me
breathing for the next few seconds,'
Sure enough, I was right.

We will look on these days with great affection.
Remember when we were in the bar talking
and the two men on the next table
stopped their conversation
rooted to every word we said.
These seem to be the things that happen now.
Let's make the most of it while it lasts.

Some days are just perfect.
Neither of us ever knew that.
They're not always Tuesdays
but that's the day cocktails are two for one.
Not that we minded when they were full price
because everything was going our way.
Weird isn't it.

The day we missed our flight
you told me to jump on your back
you spread out your arms and made the plane noise
N'yaaaaaaaaaaaaaaaaaaaaaaaawwwwwwww.
and somehow we made it.

We are dodging bullets now,
we're weaving through the spray from machine guns,
all you need to do is put your hand on my shoulder
and I'll shout "Run!"
Or the other way round.
It doesn't matter which
and that's the best thing of all.

And I know that when I inevitably go crazy
and take hostages
you will be out there with a megaphone.

A poem for Simon Armitage

Simon, I work at Anglia Windows
and no-one there has heard of you.
You weren't on the GCSE syllabus
when we were at school.
That's why I've been hiding bits of your poems
around the office
like treasure hunt clues.

Now people find you in filing cabinets
your couplets scribbled in the margins
of company reports
symbolism on spreadsheets
half rhymes in ring binders.

I quote lines of your best poems
when I'm replying to group emails
it makes it much less tedious.
I've seen the girl I sit next to smiling
appreciating one of your similes
I set as her screensaver
whenever she went to the toilet.

I've even been outside.
I chalked entire stanzas in the car park
I hope this does not infringe on copyright.

I hacked into the Anglia Intranet:
people from the Technical Department
now find samples of your new collection
where installation procedures used to be.
Alan Medlicott is going to be furious.

And I know the people I work with
won't go to Waterstones
to buy the complete works of Simon Armitage
but it might give someone something to think about
when they're at home at night
making tomorrow's sandwiches.

A day in the life

Midnight
Me and Kelly are in Take Five.
The barman calls time
he looks at us and winks.

1 am
The landlord has his coat on
we sip our whiskies and leave.

2 am
Kelly knows a bar that's still serving.
We sit in the corner. No-one knows our names.

3 am
I walk Kelly to her front door. This is romance.
I ask to borrow money for a taxi home.
This is realism.

4 am
Trying to get to sleep knowing your alarm is set for seven
is like being on a delayed train
worrying about your connection.

5 am
I dream I am drumming with The Beatles
John Lennon high fives me
holds the limousine door open for me.

6 am
All my life I have been waking before the alarm
waiting for the beeps.

7 am
I wee and brush my teeth simultaneously.
This is saving valuable seconds.

8 am
Walking to work I think about phoning in sick

9 am
The country is full of people logging on
adjusting swivel chairs
deleting bulk email.

10 am
There is a lady here whose job is to make us coffee,
photocopy,
leave bottles out for the milkman.

11 am
Kelly texts

'still in bed
x'

12 pm
An email challenges me to name bald footballers.
I get seven before resorting to Google.

1 pm
In Spain this would be siesta time
back to our homes for Sangria and sleep.
Stewart from Sales has got a nosebleed.

2 pm
I am asked to sign a birthday card
for someone I have never met.

3 pm
A team meeting
an oval table
in the centre a plate of biscuits
that no-one can reach.

4 pm
Waiting for the clock to turn.
I do a poo so I don't have to go
in my own time.

5 pm
I am out the door like a Japanese bullet train.

6 pm
I walk to Burger King
tomorrow I will start a fitness regime
couscous and swimming.

7 pm
On the kitchen notice board
takeaway menus are displayed
like treasured family photographs.

8 pm
I power shower the knots in my neck
Imperial Leather my balls and armpits.

9 pm
Kelly comes round.
When the doorbell rings
I realise I have no socks on.

10 pm
In the pub a couple have a stand up row.
We watch it like they're on Trisha.

11 pm
I do my impression of Del Boy falling through the bar.

Midnight
Me and Kelly in Take Five
the barman calls time
he looks at us and winks.

The continuity announcer stole my wife

We were on our second bottle of wine
when she went quiet, then said: "I've been cheating on you."
Just then the doorbell rang. It was our takeaway.

The man kept ringing the bell
he must have known we were in
but this was no time for chow mein.
"Is it with someone I know?" I asked
"Sort of," she said. "You know the bloke who says things like
And now, the snooker
and Next on BBC 2: *Eggheads*. It's him."

She said it had been going on for two years
and I thought about all the times we'd been on the settee
waiting for Masterchef to start
and she didn't even flinch.
I hadn't suspected a thing.
I know she went away with work sometimes
but then so did I. I still feel guilty about the time
I drank everything in the mini-bar
and called up a chatline
but all the time she was shagging the BBC2 continuity announcer.
I bet when he was saying "Next, *Later with Jools Holland*,"
he was thinking about her tits.

"Not the bloke on Dave?" my friend said when I told him.
"BBC 2,"I said and he nodded like it was Eton.
"Is he the bloke who says And now, Eggheads?" he asked.
He said "Do you think he has to wear a shirt and tie,
when he does his announcing,
or can he just wear something comfy like a jumper?
Do you think he just sits in a room with a TV and a microphone?
Do you think he can say what he wants,
or does he have to follow a script?"

There were so many questions I didn't have an answer to.
We didn't eat our takeaway
just threw the thin plastic bag in the bin.
She went upstairs, packed her bags and left
and I always hoped she would come back
but she never did. And now whenever I watch BBC 2
I think how happy she must be
with the continuity announcer.
I still don't even know what he looks like.

I wish I believed in aliens

I walk along Brighton beach
the sky is beautiful tonight, fresh, and the moon
is not quite full.
It's gibbous. The best one.
There are so many stars and it's on nights like this
I wish I believed in aliens,
that I could look up at the night sky
and there was a chance I'd see a flying saucer.
Little green men waving hello,
shining a beam for me to climb on board.
And my God we'd see some things,
I'd slag off my fellow earthlings
as we hurtled towards a black hole.

I wish that before I closed my bedroom curtains every night
I could allow myself to check for asteroids crashing towards us.
I wish I had the imagination to say
"This world is not safe from our alien overlords!"
That one day the man in the bank will rip off his face
unveil three heads
and suddenly everything would make sense.

If only I could believe there is a parallel universe,
worlds of infinite doppelgangers;
that at the other end of the Milky Way

there is a man identical to me but is left handed
and loves Marmite
and doesn't have to borrow money from his mum.

I wish I didn't find it so implausible that a spaceship
could land beside me on Brighton beach,
sea monsters could poke their heads out of the water,
that far off seagulls are pterodactyls.
I wish I could wake up one morning surrounded by mist
in my underpants at Jodrell Bank
with no idea how I got there.
That's why I look up at the Brighton night sky and scream:

"Take me! Do with me what you will!"
But deep down I know they won't come
and I have to accept that my imagination
is as extinct as dinosaurs.
It's not been the same since the Christmas Eve
when I saw my dad dressed as Santa Claus.

Both Grandmas

Both his grandmas died on the same day.
He got one phone call
then half an hour later the phone rang again.
As he planned the logistics with his A-Z

he remembered the year he spent
cheating on his girlfriend,
the Christmas Day he ate two turkey dinners
and wasn't even full.

Apocalypse

I was fairly sure this was the Apocalypse.
Earthquakes, tidal waves, the leaders of nations going nuts,
and have you noticed how windy it's been lately.
Birds were falling from the sky in Connecticut
and I was sure that next it would be the sky
belly flopping onto us.

That's why I've been walking up and down the road
wearing my *The End is Nigh* sandwich board
ringing my bell.
"And don't even start me on Osama," I say to a man
who stops me to shake my hand.

"What else are the government keeping from us?"
I shout through a megaphone, asking passers by
to sign my clipboard.
Didn't those Twin Towers crumple suspiciously?
What about those flags, blowing the wrong way
on the footage of the 'moon landings'?

Planets will align into the shape of a cross
there will be rivers of blood.
"We're all in this together!"
I tell a guy who knows what I'm talking about.
We agree it will be seminal,

like Hendrix at Woodstock,
that out of all the people who have ever lived, we are the chosen ones
who will be around when the world crumbles like an Oxo cube.
It makes up for being too young for the cinema release
of *Return of the Jedi*.

"The dead will rise from their graves," I tell an old lady
who is interested in the pamphlets I am handing out at the cemetery.
"Are you sure?" she asks
and I catch a reflection of myself in her sunglasses
and realise I want Armageddon a bit too much:
it would be convenient
tie up a few loose ends
and I could persuade myself something huge had been imminent
if it hadn't been for that bloody Apocalypse.

Je joue le pingpong

I have plunged the cafetiere.
I have phoned in sick to watch the cricket
I'm listening to *Rubber Soul*
a different Beatles album every day.
I'm thinking about writing a blog.

I've got a big telly.
I watch it and I like it.

I'm waving at a helicopter
I'm trying on hats in the mirror
thank-you for lending me your bicycle.

People try and overanalyse things
they discuss whether Bob Dylan is a lyricist or a poet.
He's Bob Dylan.

I like croissants, jam, that kind of thing.
Sometimes the film is better than the book.
I would like to hit in the face the dressed-for-tennis America man.
You never feel more alive than when hiding under a bed.

Whoopee cushion under unsuspecting bottom!
All the sandwiches in Boots are reduced!
Even the posh ones!

Last night there was this drunk guy in my street shouting
he was with a girl who kept telling him to be quiet
and I don't know what it is
that makes someone rant like that in the rain
but something good in life has disappeared
and is lost forever.

I went to a gallery. I saw a painting and I liked it.
If you occasionally say something in French
it will make you seem more interesting.
"I wonder what he means
when he says some people overanalyse things?"

I am eating a lolly with my top off.
Je joue le pingpong.
I like *Juno*. It's good.

Stolen rum tastes better.
Let's not talk about the air guitar lamp incident
or the kiss-on-both-cheeks fail.

A secret something

You whispered sex things in my ear
took my hand
we both switched our phones off
then on again the next morning
and my bedroom walls echoed with the *beep beep beeps*
of people wondering where we were.

That day at work it was like nothing had happened
apart from an occasional glance and smile.
You told me that next time you would make breakfast
because my bacon had been too crispy.

For the next month, we spoke in this exciting secret language.
It was like the two of us had murdered someone;
I'd accidentally tripped an electrician down the stairs
and now he was in a bin bag in the boot of your car.
The only thing we knew for certain: we were in this together.

"You do know this can't continue?" you said,
"because of all this."
You gestured at the open plan office
but when I turned to look it seemed all our colleagues
had rearranged their chairs into the shape of a love heart.

Everyone thinks they know you so well
but I have seen your iTunes
and we have shared those bacon sandwich mornings
where you've told me things they will never know
that you love miniature railways,
your grandad drove steam trains and since he passed away
you've found yourself reading and rereading the books

he specifically requested were left to you in his will.
You and your now fully recovered brother go on trips to stations
of significance for railway enthusiasts
and when you told me these stories I wanted to consume you.
It was like going on Amazon
to buy an entire seven season HBO box set
on the basis of a promising trailer.
Do you want this product gift wrapped?
More than you could ever possibly believe.

That's why I'm so glad we killed that electrician.
Maybe he'll become a martyr for our domestic bliss.
He is still in the boot
and will probably be there for a while.
Neither of us has the heart to dump his body in the river
dig a hole in the woods
because right now, we just like things the way they are.

The boy and girl busking on Hastings seafront.

Please promise me you will be a famous band.
We need this, the three of us.
You for Jack Daniels in hotel rooms
me so that I can tell anyone who will listen
that I saw them when they were just kids
busking in their checked shirts.

I'd remember how I was looking for a post box
and just stopped in my tracks when I saw them,
felt compelled to give them everything
from the zip bit of my wallet.
That I've never given away money before or since
but I felt so drawn towards these two
who I could tell weren't brother and sister
or boyfriend and girlfriend
just the only two in their class with vinyl collections,
they both had dads who liked Dylan
and my God they were skinny.

So dear boy and girl busking on Hastings seafront,
please don't give up.
Recently I met a retired lighthouse keeper
who said that every day in that lighthouse he regretted
not trying harder to be a footballer when he was younger.

He'd been strong and tall for his age and couldn't play a game
without someone's dad telling him
he should have trials with Wolves
or West Brom, or Villa.
He lived in the Midlands
became a builder
and started drinking.

There were a few of us watching these two teenagers
busking in the rain. Playing guitars. Singing.
And these were no bollocks cover versions. These were tunes,
tunes, good haircuts
and an upturned trilby full of pound coins
enough to buy a new amp.
And when they whispered to each other in-between songs
making each other laugh,
each one of us would have queued
all the way down the promenade
to have swapped places with them.

Once I went to a restaurant in Weston-super-Mare
and I left without paying.
I hadn't planned to, but at the end of the meal
I just thought 'Sod waiting for the bill' and stood up,
put my coat on
and strolled out like I owned the South West.
It wasn't until I switched my bedroom light out that night
I realised that somewhere I'd given up on life.

Which is why when I saw this boy and girl
busking on Hastings seafront
I couldn't help myself picturing the garage they rehearsed in.
They'd practise every other Thursday at seven thirty.
Sometimes one of them would say "I've written a new song,"
sit up on the chest freezer and play it
while the other listened
sitting on a rocking horse that was in there for storage
for some time it might be useful in the future.

The 2009 Cannes film festival

I am the only one still alive
from that orgy at the 2009 Cannes Film Festival.
David and his redhead wife
were killed in a car crash two weeks later,
the Assistant Director of Photography
died in a warehouse fire last Christmas,
and Caroline never had the chance to give up smoking.

The girl with the piercings: malaria.
And the actor you've probably seen in things
had his obituary in Thursday's *Guardian*.
"Known for his love of champagne," the piece began
and as I read I could picture him standing there
his hands on his hips.

Soya milk

I heard someone making sure
their tea was served with soya milk.
At the time I was very aware

there wasn't a single interesting thing about me
so I decided to always insist
I only drank tea made with soya.

I looked forward to saying "I can't drink this!"
I'd spit out a mouthful over someone's new carpet
saying "This isn't fucking soya!"

No cows teets for me. No UHT.
You wouldn't expect a vegetarian
to gnaw on a shoulder of pork.

If I am invited to someone's house I don't RSVP
people don't know whether to expect me.
"We better get some soya," they say

"just in case."

Schmoozing at an evening do

No-one really wants canapés
but they are a useful device to disguise social discomfort.
Taking a smoked haddock fishcake from the waitress's silver tray
is essentially the same as checking for texts.

Glasses of fizz are marginally more welcome
you calculate how quickly you can reasonably polish one off
before reaching out for another.
In this minute or so you can forget you are all by yourself,
that you have no-one to talk to
and soon enough the person making their speech
will be making their speech
or the band will start

or someone you actually like will turn up
or it will be late enough to go home
without it seeming rude.
But for now you are stuck
with a lemon and black pepper scallop
clinging to an empty glass

because life is a constant dilemma of wondering
what to do with our hands.

A pair of last year's trousers

Elderly Shopkeeper Apprehends Armed Robber.
Cat Walks Seventy Miles To Find Previous Owners.
Politician Leaves Dossier In Brothel.
But no story is better than the Slimmer of the Year
holding up a pair of last year's trousers
being told to smile for local press.

Everybody loves these novelty articles:
the World's Shortest Man, sextuplets, Guy Goma,
but nothing comes close to someone who used to be well fat
and is now thin (ish).
Tabloid readers are astonished by the photograph
taken last year in his swimming trunks in his paddling pool
for his poorly attended fortieth.

He tells Matthew Wright on Channel 5
that was the day he started Googling diets.
He shakes his head at the memory of the patio chair
snapping in two beneath him.
You can imagine the euphoria
of those trousers getting slacker.
54 inches. 52 inches. Incremental thinning.

And even though he will never wear them again
I hope he never throws away those fat jeans,

that they stay hanging in the wardrobe
like an ice hockey shirt given by a Canadian cousin.
They are a souvenir of a year spent eating Philadelphia Light
on water biscuits,
changing the route home from work
to avoid that KFC.

Sometimes in life there is no-one to help you
you have to do things by yourself.
A photograph saying any of us can achieve anything:
the Slimmer of the Year
holding up a pair of last year's trousers.

Listening to Radio 3 in the bath

I fill the bath with Rosemary and Eucalyptus Radox,
dunk my head and allow my shoulders to collapse,

nudge the hot water tap with my big toe
take a sip from my glass of Merlot.

I have missed the party by now
this was supposed to be a quick in and out

but sometimes I'm happy to close my eyes, listen to Radio 3.
I look at my hands. I am starting to get wrinkly.

Our waitress is Employee of the Month

Her photograph is in the foyer
and I imagine her pretending not to be bothered
when it was announced at the team meeting,
a semi-circle of applause.

But the next morning she'd have shown her mum
the Twenty Pound High Street Voucher
and her mum would have said "Well done," and meant it,
because she knows it's important
to appreciate the small things.

And in town our waitress will have gone from shop to shop
content she didn't have to start work until half seven.
Trying on a maxi dress in River Island
she'd wonder whether it was for the time
she helped an amputee cut up his food

managing to strike the perfect balance between being too fussy
and pretending she hadn't noticed.
She didn't even need to say anything like
"Shall I help you with that?"

it was just this intuition
she didn't even realise she had.
And as she helped chop up his gammon and potatoes
he told her he was in town to see his daughter

who had just proposed to her boyfriend
taking advantage of the leap year
and he was so nervous he wouldn't get on with his future son-in-law.
Our waitress would have asked if he'd like a dessert,

and at first he'd have said no
but she'd have said "Oh, go on!"
because she knows it's important to appreciate the small things.
She'd have smiled as he scooped up the last of his custard.

Our table is ready. The four of us take our seats
and as she hands out the menus
puts serviettes on our knees, she must know that we know,
we'd been in the foyer for so long, staring at her photograph

and I think: Please, no-one say anything,
don't let it be like the time we saw Dame Judi Dench
get out of a taxi by the Old Vic and shouted "Judi! Judi!"
until she turned and waved so awkwardly.

Let's just be grateful we're being served by the Employee of the Month
and as she carries our plates of sea bass
we know that if any of us start to choke on a bone
we will feel her arm around us.

65

Acknowledgements

These poems have appeared in publications including: *The Guardian, The Spectator, The Big Issue, Rialto, Fuselit, Barbara.*

I'd like to thank: Tim Clare, Tony Cook at ABC Tales, Laura Dockrill, Joe Dunthorne, Chris Gomm, Chris Hicks, Kirstie Irving, Patrick Lappin, Yanny Mac, Molly Naylor, Sam Ratcliffe, Sally Roe, Joel Stickley, Ross Sutherland, Hannah Walker, Rebecca Winfield, Luke Wright.

Special thanks to my mum, dad and Karen.

Also by **NASTY LITTLE PRESS**

Pub Stuntman
by Tim Clare
ISBN: 978-0-9573000-0-2 | £10

100 Ways To Write Badly Well
by Joel Sticklet
ISBN: 978-0-9573000-1-9 | £10

Boring The Arse Off Young People
by Martin Figura
ISBN: 978-0-9563767-3-2 | £5

Under The Pier
by Salena Godden
ISBN: 978-0-9563767-4-9 | £5

Mostly Dreich
by Elvis McGonagall
ISBN: 978-0-9573000-2-6

Small Talk
by Nic Aubury
ISBN: 978-0-9563767-9-4 | £5

nastylittlepress.org